TRISTAN PIPERSON

# Lake Louise Travel Guide

*Discover all the best attractions, activities, restaurants, hotels and insider tips for visiting Lake Louise, Canada*

Copyright © 2023 by Tristan Piperson

All rights reserved. No part of this publication may be reproduced, stored or transmitted in any form or by any means, electronic, mechanical, photocopying, recording, scanning, or otherwise without written permission from the publisher. It is illegal to copy this book, post it to a website, or distribute it by any other means without permission.

Tristan Piperson asserts the moral right to be identified as the author of this work.

Tristan Piperson has no responsibility for the persistence or accuracy of URLs for external or third-party Internet Websites referred to in this publication and does not guarantee that any content on such Websites is, or will remain, accurate or appropriate.

Designations used by companies to distinguish their products are often claimed as trademarks. All brand names and product names used in this book and on its cover are trade names, service marks, trademarks and registered trademarks of their respective owners. The publishers and the book are not associated with any product or vendor mentioned in this book. None of the companies referenced within the book have endorsed the book.

First edition

This book was professionally typeset on Reedsy.
Find out more at reedsy.com

# Contents

| | | |
|---|---|---|
| 1 | Introduction | 1 |
| 2 | Packing for Your Visit and Things to Know Before Visiting | 2 |
| 3 | Banff National Park Pass | 4 |
| 4 | Parking | 6 |
| 5 | Shuttle | 9 |
| 6 | Lake Louise Visitor Center | 10 |
| 7 | Hotels in Lake Louise | 11 |
| 8 | Super Markets | 18 |
| 9 | Hiking | 19 |
| 10 | Horseback Riding | 24 |
| 11 | Boating | 26 |
| 12 | Summer Gondola | 28 |
| 13 | Skiing and Snowboarding | 30 |
| 14 | Ice Skating | 32 |
| 15 | Ice Magic Festival | 34 |
| 16 | Dog Sledding | 36 |
| 17 | Enjoying the Wildlife | 38 |
| 18 | Visiting the Fairmont Chateau Lake Louise | 47 |
| 19 | Restaurants | 49 |
| 20 | Sunrise Over Lake Louise | 55 |
| 21 | Conclusion | 57 |
| 22 | Resources | 58 |

# 1

# Introduction

Lake Louise is a glacial lake located in Banff National Park in Alberta, Canada. It is a beautiful and magical place that is sure to leave you with lasting memories. It is known for its stunning scenery, turquoise waters, and majestic surrounding mountains. It is one of the most popular tourist destinations in all of Canada and is often referred to as the Jewel of Canada. It is located 3.1 miles west of the Hamlet of Lake Louise and the Trans-Canada Highway (Highway 1). The lake is located just behind the iconic Fairmont Chateau Lake Louise, at an elevation of 5,249 feet. Lake Louise is about 2 miles long, 1 mile wide and is 230 feet at its deepest. The lake is fed by the Victoria Glacier, and its stunning turquoise color is caused by the presence of rock flour, which is a fine-grained sediment that is carried into the lake by the glacier. Words cannot adequately describe how beautiful Lake Louise is, it is a truly breathtaking destination. Lake Louise is a world-renowned destination for its stunning scenery, pristine waters, and abundance of activities. Whether you're looking for a relaxing getaway or an adrenaline-pumping adventure, you're sure to find something to love at Lake Louise. With a little planning, you can have a safe and enjoyable visit.

# 2

# Packing for Your Visit and Things to Know Before Visiting

There are a few things you will need to bring with you if you are planning a visit to Lake Louise:

- A valid passport or other form of identification
- A park pass for Banff National Park
- Comfortable shoes or hiking boots
- A jacket or sweater, even in the summer
- Sunscreen, sunglasses, and a hat
- A camera to capture the stunning scenery
- A sense of adventure!

Here are some additional tips for visiting Lake Louise:

- Book your accommodations in advance, especially if you are visiting during the peak season (June-August).
- Arrive early in the morning or late in the evening to avoid the crowds.
- Decide in advance how you will get to Lake Louise from your

PACKING FOR YOUR VISIT AND THINGS TO KNOW BEFORE VISITING

accommodation; take your own car (parking is VERY limited) or take a shuttle bus
- Be prepared for the weather to change quickly. VERY quickly
- Take your time and enjoy the scenery.
- Be respectful of the environment.

# 3

# Banff National Park Pass

Lake Louise is located within Banff National Park and in order to enter Banff National Park you need to have a Banff National Park pass. There are a few different ways to get a pass for Banff National Park:

- Online: You can purchase a pass online at the Parks Canada website. Just remember to pack the pass in your suitcase and take it with you on your trip. If you accidentally leave your pass at home you will be required to buy an additional pass for entry into the park. You can request a refund for the "duplicate" pass but you must keep all of your receipts to submit with the original pass for a refund. Buying the pass ahead of time allows you to drive right into the park and bypass the line (sometimes the line is short, other times it is long) of cars waiting to buy their pass.
- At the gate: You can also purchase a pass at the gate of Banff National Park. This option eliminates the risk of forgetting your pass at home but it does require you to wait online at the gate to buy your pass. Depending upon the season, time of day, and luck this could take a while.

## BANFF NATIONAL PARK PASS

- At the visitor center: You can also purchase a pass at the visitor center in Banff and at the visitor center in Lake Louise.

At the time of this writing there are two basic options for park passes: Day Pass or Discovery Pass. A Day Pass gives you entry into the park for one day and the Discovery Pass gives you unlimited access to all of Canada's National Parks, national marine conservation areas, and national historic sites for an entire year from the date of purchase. If you are going to be spending more than a few days in Lake Louise and if you are planning on visiting any other National Parks in Canada the Discovery Pass will save you money and is the best value.

Within these two categories, Day Pass and Discovery Pass, are sub categories: adult, senior, or family. The cost of a pass will vary depending on the type of pass you purchase. A daily pass for adults is $10.50, a senior pass is $9, a family pass is $21. An annual Discovery Pass for an adult is $72.25, a senior is $61.75, and a family is $145.25.

Once you have purchased a pass, you will need to display it in your vehicle when you enter Banff National Park. You can display the pass on your dashboard or on the rearview mirror.

# 4

# Parking

P arking at Lake Louise is a challenge, especially during the peak summer season. There are not very many places to park your car near the lake and they fill up VERY early.

# PARKING

The most convenient option is to park in the main parking lot, which is located just a short walk from the lake. This lot is $12.25 per vehicle per day and is open from 7am to 7pm. However, this fills up very quickly and as most people spend the majority of the day at Lake Louise, spots do not open up very often.

If the main parking lot is full, you can try parking in one of the overflow lots. These lots are located a short drive from the lake and are free to park in. However, they can be quite a walk from the lake, so be prepared for a hike.

You can also try parking at the Lake Louise Park and Ride, which is located about 5 kilometers from the lake. The Park and Ride is free to park in and there is a shuttle that runs every 15 minutes to the lake.

Here are some additional tips for parking at Lake Louise:

- Arrive early. The best way to guarantee a parking spot is to arrive early.
- Plan on spending the night in the town of Lake Louise as opposed to Banff. The town of Lake Louise is about a 10 minute drive to parking at the lake whereas the drive from Banff is closer to 45 minutes. This will make it easier for you to get to the parking lots early, aim for 7am for your best chance to get a parking spot.
- Consider using the Park and Ride. The Park and Ride is free to park in and there is a shuttle that runs every 15 minutes to the lake.
- Be prepared for a hike. If you park in the overflow lots, be prepared for a long walk to the lake.
- Be prepared for crowds. Lake Louise is a popular tourist destination, so be prepared for crowds, especially during the peak season.
- Consider visiting Lake Louise in the evening for sunset. In the summer, the sun usually sets around 9pm and most people leave the park around 6pm or 7pm. Meaning parking spaces should open up and paid parking is only required from 7am until 7pm, so if you

were to arrive at 7pm, you have a good chance of finding a parking spot and the parking will be free. While you will not have much time to see the Lake you will get to see an incredible sunset and the park should be much less crowded!

# 5

## Shuttle

If the thought of taking your car to Lake Louise seems like a possible liability to you, not to worry there is a shuttle. Parks Canada operates a Park and Ride shuttle but you need to book it online in advance. There is also a public bus system (ROAM Transit) that's available. Both of these options will save you from the hassle and stress of worrying over the parking situation and are available for a small fee.

# 6

# Lake Louise Visitor Center

It may seem obvious, but one of the first places you may want to stop at is the Lake Louise Visitor Center. It is located at 201 Village Road. The staff at the visitor center are extremely helpful and knowledgeable. If you have any questions or are looking for recommendations this is the place for you. They also have a variety of exhibits and programs that teach visitors about the local history and culture. It is a rich history and the staff has great stories!

# 7

# Hotels in Lake Louise

Staying in Lake Louise is not to be missed. The beauty and majesty of the area is absolutely breathtaking and will stay with you always. There are not many hotels in Lake Louise so you will want to book your stay in advance. Here are some of the best options for hotels in Lake Louise:

The Fairmont Chateau Lake Louise

This is the hotel you think of when you think of Lake Louise. It is iconic and gorgeous. It has the BEST location, the BEST views and is literally right on Lake Louise. The Fairmont Chateau Lake Louise is the epitome of luxury and is the premier choice. It is also, by far, the most expensive resort. Not only is it the most expensive hotel in Lake Louise but it is the most expensive in all of Banff. The rates for rooms are very high. You are paying for the location. And for the views. Their dining room offers some of the absolute best views of Lake Louise and while you do not need to be staying at the Fairmont Chateau Lake Louise to get a reservation at the restaurant, preference is given to guests of the restaurant and the premier tables (best views) are reserved for hotel guests.

On-site amenities include an indoor pool, hot tub, steam room, and fitness area with a stretching room.The resort has a full spa which offers massages, wraps, body scrubs, and facials. The hotel also manages the ice skating rink and the ice bar (in winter). An additional perk of staying at the Fairmont Chateau Lake Louise is that you do not have to deal with the stressful parking situation. Parking is available for guests of the resort for an additional fee.

There is, however, a potential downside to staying at the Fairmont Chateau Lake Louise. It is crowded and very busy. As it is the ONLY hotel actually on Lake Louise and really the only hotel that is close to Lake Louise, buses and shuttles are constantly driving up to it and departing from it. The outside area is very crowded with tourists arriving and getting ready to set out to explore the amazing area. Things do calm down in the evening but during the day it can be a bit overwhelming. This hotel has the best location and saves you from wasting your vacation time and worrying over where to park your car, but you pay for this and it will be very crowded.

## Paradise Lodge and Bungalows

This hotel has probably the second best location, and is one of the best hotels in Lake Louise. It is about ¼ of a mile walk from the lake and is a great option for those not wanting to pay the exorbitant rate at the Fairmont Chateau. Additionally, this hotel is nowhere near as busy and much calmer and quieter than the fairmont Chateau. This hotel is only open during the summer season and is also quite calm and not as busy as the Fairmont.

## Post Hotel and Spa

This is a luxury resort and is a much loved and favored hotel in Lake Louise. It is beautifully situated among pristine woods with magnificent views of the surrounding mountains. It is certified Relais & Chateaux and is known for its fine dining and having one of the largest wine cellars (25,000 bottles).

## Moraine Lake Lodge

This is a beautiful hotel with a lot to offer guests. The hotel is picturesque and the setting and views are spectacular. It is located right on Moraine Lake and is an extremely popular hotel. The Lodge is really a series of bungalows and it is a fantastic option for families. Additionally, guests of the hotel are allowed to park in the parking lot. This is a HUGE perk as parking can be very difficult. And, guests of the hotel are allowed to take out a canoe on Lake Moraine at no cost! Canoeing on Lake Moraine and Lake Louise are arguably the most popular activities in the region and rates for non-guests are $120 an hour. This hotel is a wonderful option.

## Baker Creek Mountain Resort

Composed of a group of cozy log cabins you can either reserve a cabin or a room. This hotel is very comfortable and is in the woods and the scenery is beautiful.

## Lake Louise Inn

The Lake Louise Inn is a great option for families. It is nestled in the woods and has beautiful views of the mountains and is located close to the gas stations, The Valley Market, and is a short drive to Lake Louise. They have mini golf, a swimming pool, and restaurants.

## HI Lake Louise Alpine Center

This hostel is very affordable and ideal for those on a tight budget. Dormitory style with a few private rooms available.

# 8

# Super Markets

If you are planning on staying in a hotel with a kitchen or just want to save some money by buying your own food at a grocery store (as opposed to eating out at a restaurant) here is what you need to know. In Lake Louise you can shop for groceries at the Village Market. It is a small grocery shop that has the essentials but is not a full blown grocery store with everything you might be looking for. If you are looking for a large grocery store your best options are to stop in Canmore or Banff to do your grocery shopping before heading to Lake Louise. In Banff, two of the most popular grocery stores are the IGA and Nester's Market. In Canmore, Save-On and Safeway are two of the larger, well stocked grocery stores.

# 9

# Hiking

Lake Louise is a hiker's paradise! Lake Louise has a variety of trails to suit all levels of experience. The scenery you will be hiking through is simply stunning. Some of the most popular hikes include:

- Mount Fairview Lookout Trail: This is probably the easiest and shortest hike at Lake Louise. It is 1.4 miles long and begins just outside of the Fairmont Chateau near the boathouse. This hike can almost be described as a walk and can easily be completed in under an hour. Most of the trail is paved and it takes you around Lake Louise and you get an incredible view of the Fairmont Chateau.

- The Lake Agnes Tea house Trail: This moderate, 2.5-mile round-trip, hike takes you to a charming tea house located in the mountains above Lake Louise. Along the way you will discover incredible sights, gorgeous views, and impressive landscapes. Be sure to keep your eyes on the lookout for wildlife while hiking! It is common to see the adorable pika darting in and out of the rocks near the Lake Agnes Tea House.

- The Plain of Six Glaciers Trail: This challenging 6.2-mile round-trip hike takes you to a viewpoint of six glaciers. This is for hikers with good stamina and some hiking experience.

- The Mirror Lake Hike: This is an easy 0.9-mile round-trip hike that takes you to a beautiful mirror lake located in the forest. It also gives you a great view of the "Big Beehive" mountain.

# HIKING

# 10

# Horseback Riding

An incredible horseback riding tour is a great way to explore and see some of the picturesque spots in Lake Louise. You decide which tour is best for your experience level and what you would like to see. From an hour-long introductory lesson to multiple days in the back country, a horseback riding tour through Lake Louise is bound to be a memorable experience. Brewsters Lake Louise Stables offer many tour options and is conveniently located a stone's throw from the Chateau.

## HORSEBACK RIDING

# 11

# Boating

Lake Louise is a popular spot for boating, with a variety of watercraft available for rent. Nothing is more quintessential Lake Louise than renting a canoe and paddling around the lake! It's a fun activity for everyone and gives you a completely different perspective on Lake Louise. Be sure to bring your camera to get incredible photos while paddling around and also be sure to get a picture of yourself paddling the canoe! Spending an hour or few hours paddling around Lake Louise is on many people's bucket list and it is easy to see why; breathtaking views, incredible colors, and the overwhelming sheer beauty of the lake make this a must do activity. You can rent canoes and kayaks. This is a VERY popular activity and the rentals are not cheap, so be forewarned. You can bring your own canoe or kayak to save you the pricey rental fee, however, this means you will need to arrive at the lake very early in order to get yourself a parking spot close enough to the lake to be able to carry your canoe.

# BOATING

# 12

## Summer Gondola

Why not take a fun ride in the Lake Louise Summer Gondola? The views are amazing and you have a very good chance of seeing some of Lake Louise's famous wildlife, including the grizzly bear! From high above, in your gondola, you will take in beautiful 360 degree views of stunning landscape. The flowers and plants and berries attract much of the natural wildlife in the area and this is one of the best ways to get to see wildlife. After your gondola ride you can grab a bite to eat on the deck and continue to take in the amazing scenery.

## SUMMER GONDOLA

# 13

## Skiing and Snowboarding

In the winter, Lake Louise transforms into a winter wonderland. Lake Louise Ski Resort is one of the most popular ski resorts in Canada, with over 4,200 feet of skier and rider accessible terrain. The trails offer spectacular views of the mountains and surrounding landscape. The elevation is 8,625 feet. The ski resort also has an impressive 4 terrain parks and a tube park. Winter time in Lake Louise is a great time to visit and skiers and riders of all ages and abilities will find there is a variety of terrain to meet their every need.

SKIING AND SNOWBOARDING

# 14

## Ice Skating

In the winter, you can also skate on the frozen surface of Lake Louise, for free. There is no better place to ice skate in Canada than at Lake Louise. Nothing is more iconic and awe inspiring than ice skating amid the towering mountains on Lake Louise. It has regularly been considered one of the world's best ice skating rinks. The Fairmont Chateau Lake Louise creates and maintains the ice skating rink on Lake Louise. This is really incredible because they clear the rink of snow everyday, allowing visitors to enjoy and use the rink in the winter, even after a heavy snow. What really sets ice skating at Lake Louise apart from the other lakes is the lake's atmosphere. Around the lake shore, you can find cozy fires, an ice bar, a horse drawn sleigh that you can ride, and even an ice castle.

# ICE SKATING

# 15

# Ice Magic Festival

The Fairmont Chateau hosts the Ice Magic Festival every January and it is something to behold. There is an international ice carving competition in the beginning of January (check for exact dates) where ice carving artists from around the world come to compete and sculpt unbelievable creations from blocks of ice in 36 hours. Don't worry if you miss the actual competition, the Fairmont Chateau leaves the sculptures up for display for weeks (weather dependent). If possible, try to see the sculptures before they are covered with snow, but either way you will be impressed and amazed! Also, if you can visit during the week it is likely to be less crowded than on the weekends.

# ICE MAGIC FESTIVAL

# 16

# Dog Sledding

Looking for a unique experience and a way to take in the majestic scenery? Try a dog sledding adventure! Kingmik Dog Sled Tours offers 2 tours in the Lake Louise area: a 30 minute tour and a 90 minute tour. It is a fantastic opportunity to see areas of Lake Louise that you probably wouldn't see otherwise and you get to learn about life with sled dogs! These tours are very popular so call in advance.

# DOG SLEDDING

# 17

# Enjoying the Wildlife

Lake Louise is home to a variety of wildlife, and if you keep your eyes and ears open you are sure to see many of them!

**Pika** Pika are adorable little critters that can usually be found among the rocks at the far end of Lake Louise and up by Lake Agnes Tea House. They are small and blend in well with the rocks they frequently dash in and out of. Be sure to listen and if you hear a high pitch squeak, stop and look around because it was most likely a pika calling out.

Hoary Marmot. Hoary Marmots are one of the largest animals in the rodent family. They love to sun bathe on top of rocks and boulders and blend in surprisingly well so keep your eyes on the lookout! They are commonly seen on the rocks along the hike The Plain of Six Glaciers.

Elk (Wapiti). Elk are fairly common and tend to hang out in large groups. They can be easily identified by their tan color with white on their rump. Please be advised that elk are some of the most dangerous animals in Lake Louise and mothers are particularly protective of their young, so please never approach them. Appreciate them from afar and enjoy being able to see them in their natural habitat.

Moose. Although rare, you could see a Moose in Lake Louise. Moose tend to favor marshy areas.

Mountain Goat. Mountain goats are incredible climbers and frequent high cliffs and ridges. If you hike the Plain of Six Glaciers keep your eyes out for the white mountain goats high up behind the Tea House.

# ENJOYING THE WILDLIFE

Lynx. The Canadian Lynx is a beautiful, elusive animal that lives in the woods in Lake Louise. Consider yourself lucky to see one. They are easily recognizable by their black tufted ears and large wide paws.

Black Bear. Black Bears are fairly common in Lake Louise and you could encounter one. Please educate yourself of bear safety before coming to Lake Louise. Black bears can be black, brown, or light cinnamon in color. They are smaller in size than grizzly bears. Under no circumstances should you ever feed a bear or approach a bear.

Grizzly Bear. Grizzly Bears do frequent the Lake Louise area and if you are lucky enough to see one you must be very respectful of their space. Grizzly bears are larger than black bears and have a hump on their backs. They are truly majestic creatures but never, ever approach one. Again, please educate yourself on bear safety before coming to Lake Louise.

# LAKE LOUISE TRAVEL GUIDE

# 18

# Visiting the Fairmont Chateau Lake Louise

Regardless if you choose to splurge and stay at the Fairmont Chateau Lake Louise you will definitely find yourself there as it is where you will need to go to access the actual lake. Why not go inside and see what all the fuss is about? There are multiple dining rooms and you can stop in for a bite to eat, walk around and see the absolutely breathtaking views from the dining hall, and just walk around the beautiful resort. If you decide to eat there, reservations are very helpful, and the best tables with the best views are reserved for resort guests; but it is still worth exploring. The Fairmont also has a few gift shops where you can buy cute souvenirs and stock up with snacks and water before you head out for the day.

Lake Louise is such a breathtaking, special place. Be sure to make a stop at the Fairmont Chateau, check out the views and enjoy.

# LAKE LOUISE TRAVEL GUIDE

# 19

# Restaurants

There are a number of good restaurants in Lake Louise ranging from very expensive to reasonable. Many of the hotels here also have a restaurant. Below are some of the most popular restaurants in Lake Louise.

Bill Peyto's Cafe. Bill Peyto's Cafe is a fantastic restaurant with something for absolutely everyone. The place is very often crowded with people waiting outside for a table, but don't let that deter you! The food is great, the prices are reasonable, the staff is super friendly, it is centrally located and family friendly. This is definitely one of the most popular restaurants in the area.

The Lakeview Lounge. This incredible restaurant is located within the Fairmont Chateau and has absolutely stunning views of the lake and surrounding mountains. The restaurant is upscale and sophisticated and the architecture is incredible. This restaurant is pricey but an absolute quintessential Lake Louise experience.

Whitehorn Bistro. This is an incredible restaurant! A very unique dining experience that you will be sure to remember. In order to get to this restaurant you must take a quick chairlift ride from the base of the Lake Louise summer gondola! Once you have arrived, sit on the patio and take in the awe inspiring views of the mountains and glacier. The menu is incredible with all farm to table and locally sourced food. This is an experience not to be missed!

Walliser Stube. The Walliser Stube is a wonderful choice for a place to stop and have a meal. It is one of the restaurants in the Fairmont Chateau and its menu will make you feel as though you are in the alps. The fondue is not to be missed and they have a wonderful wine bar.

The Station Restaurant. This is a great restaurant in Lake Louise. The staff is extremely friendly and the food is wonderful. This is an actual former train station and there are railway cars and all sorts of authentic items from its former life as a railway station.

The Lake Louise Village Grill. This restaurant is centrally located and a great place to go if you are looking for a casual environment to grab a burger and a beer. It is family friendly and very relaxed. The service is not always super fast but you have great views to distract yourself with if you find they are busy. Relax, take a moment to eat, have a drink and enjoy the views.

RESTAURANT
EXPERIENCE Lake Louise
PUBLIC WASHROOMS
TOILETTES PUBLIQUES

## 20

## Sunrise Over Lake Louise

Lake Louise is breathtakingly beautiful and it is easy to understand why it is called the Jewel of Canada! It is an incredible place to visit all seasons of the year and it never disappoints. One of my best tips for an absolutely memorable experience is to wake up early one morning, go to Lake Louise, and take pictures of the sunrise. It is truly an extraordinary experience and the photos you will take will be incredible.

This is a popular activity, and remember parking is scarce, so you will need to wake up early. You should aim to arrive at the Lake Louise parking lot at 4:15 am. As awful as that may sound to some, it does come with some perks. You will have a parking space, and that is huge. You can go back to sleep in your car and grab a little extra rest (you might want to bring a pillow and a blanket), just be sure to set your alarm to wake you up in time to get situated and enjoy and watch the sunrise. It is not uncommon to see other photographers asleep in their cars, waiting for the sunrise. Remember, it will be significantly colder that early in the morning, bring extra clothes, hats and jackets to keep you warm while you wait. Also bring a flashlight or a headlamp. When choosing a location to set up and watch and photograph the sunrise be sure to be respectful of other photographers and do not get in their way. This can also be a fantastic people watching experience; oftentimes people come dressed up in ball gowns or extremely fashionable designer dresses to get "that perfect" photo for their social media account!

# 21

# Conclusion

Enjoy your time in Lake Louise! Lake Louise is world-renowned destination for its stunning scenery, pristine waters, and abundance of activities. No matter how you choose to spend your time in this very special place, relaxing and soaking in the scenery or traversing the intense terrain, I know it will be memorable and stay with you forever. I hope you found this book helpful and if you did, I would greatly appreciate it if you could leave a favorable review on Amazon. Thank you.

# 22

# Resources

Wikipedia contributors. (2023, February 9). *Lake Louise, Alberta*. Wikipedia. Retrieved April 25, 2023, from https://en.wikipedia.org/wiki/Lake_Louise,_Alberta

Trip to Canada: online road trip planner. (n.d.). Authentik Canada. https://www.authentikcanada.com/ca-en

Canada Landing Page - Destinationlesstravel. (2023, April 11). *How to Get Parking at Lake Louise - 2023 Guidelines & Parking Info*. Destinationless Travel. https://destinationlesstravel.com/parking-at-lake-louise/

*Lake Louise Visitor Centre*. (n.d.). https://www.travelalberta.com/listings/lake-louise-visitor-information-centre-2623

Kingmik Dogsled Tours. (n.d.). *Kingmik Dogsled Tours*. https://kingmikdogsledtours.com/

*Fairmont Hotels and Resorts - Luxury hotels*. (n.d.).

# RESOURCES

https://www.fairmont.com/

*Basecamp Resorts | Canadian Boutique Resorts and Hotels.* (n.d.). https://basecampresorts.com/

Made in the USA
Columbia, SC
18 February 2025